Prayer That Makes a Difference

Janet Clark Shay

Sable Creek
PRESS
SableCreekPress.com

Cover and text design by Diane King, dkingdesigner.com

Scripture taken from the King James Version. Public domain.

Published by Sable Creek Press.

www.sablecreekpress.com

ISBN: 978-0-9974953-1-7

Printed in the United States of America.

Dedicated to
the memory of
Joy Van Gelderen Hirth
(1956–2010),
who of all the
grandchildren was
the most like her
grandmother and
the first of those
grandchildren to be
reunited with her
grandmother in heaven.

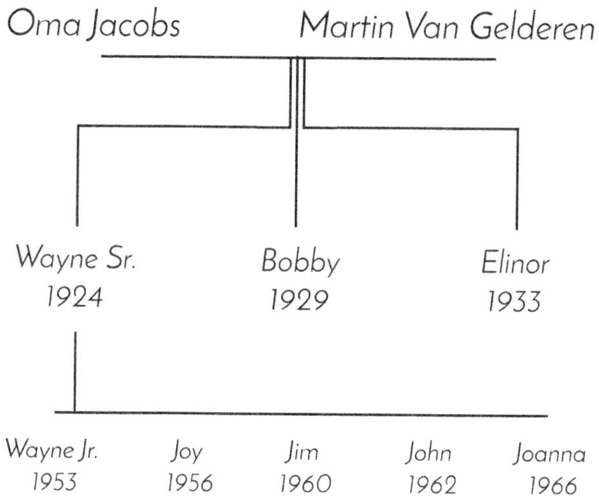
Oma Jacobs
Martin Van Gelderen
Wayne Sr.
1924
Bobby
1929
Elinor
1933
Wayne Jr.
1953
Joy
1956
Jim
1960
John
1962
Joanna
1966

Contents

Pray Confidently

—

I have called upon
thee, for thou wilt hear
me, O God: incline
thine ear unto me,
and hear my speech.

—Psalm 17:6

The Introduction

Oma Van Gelderen's biography belongs to the Van Gelderen family and those who knew and loved Oma. Her daughter, Elinor, contributed numerous accounts of her mother's life. Oma's grandson Jim's generous face-to-face interview, the personal stories recorded by Wayne Jr. and Jim, and childhood memories shared by granddaughter Joy all helped to bring life to this story. Dr. Al C. Janney, Mrs. Alvin (Jackie) Dark, and close friend Gloria Cain also contributed memorable incidents. I most especially thank Oma's youngest grandson, John, and his wife, Mary Lynn. I met John and Mary Lynn in 2002 when he held an evangelistic meeting in Arizona. That is when God first sowed the seed in my heart to look further into this woman's remarkable prayer ministry.

I have included John Van Gelderen's message, "Three Connected Truths Concerning Prayer," as an integral part of the book. It isn't enough to share life experiences. Everyone has them. It is important to understand that Oma's experiences are based on the Word of God, and I believe that John's sermon supports this truth.

The story of Oma Van Gelderen is not meant to glorify a woman or a family. Oma's story is written to encourage all Christians who desire a close communion with God and an effective prayer life that they can have both. They can experience the same miraculous intervention by God that Oma saw, once they come to understand God's plan in the matter of prayer. Oma was by no means the first Christian to have a significant prayer ministry. There are Christians throughout history who have been fervent prayer warriors. There are many yet to come. It is a privilege to share the story of one of them.

The prayer ministry of Oma Van Gelderen extended beyond her family. While you may wonder if Oma spent all of her time praying only for her loved ones, the many family examples here are given primarily because they were passed down and, in some instances, even recorded in writing. Unfortunately, most of the stories involving the many, many others outside of the Van Gelderen family were not recorded and have died with the recipients. Oma's was not a self–centered prayer ministry meant only for those closest to her, although the scope and persistence of her prayers for her family made a significant difference in their lives, and their ministries continue to make a difference for God to this day.

This book is just a small part of Oma Van Gelderen's vibrant prayer life. Only the Lord knows to what extent he used her life to honor and glorify him. May you be challenged and encouraged to seek a personal and ongoing relationship in prayer with God. Our families need intercessors. Our country needs intercessors. Our world needs intercessors.

Pray Persistently

The righteous cry, and
the LORD heareth,
and delivereth them out
of all their troubles.
—Psalm 34:17

The Person

DADEVILLE, ALABAMA 1896

Mrs. Jacobs stepped down off the porch of her humble wood-frame farmhouse and headed for the chicken coop, leaving baby Oma tucked safely in her crib and three-year-old Monka playing inside the house. As the girls' mother scattered feed to her brood of chickens, she heard a voice within her. "Go back." She didn't take it seriously at first, but soon the impression became so compelling she couldn't shake it. She abandoned the chickens and rushed back to the house.

"No!" Mrs. Jacobs screamed at the sight of baby Oma's crib. The mattress was aflame. She snatched the infant from her bed, laid her safely out of reach, and then grabbed heavy rags to smother the flames. She was still shaking long after the fire was out. She guessed that little Monka had caused the near-fatal tragedy—probably by poking a long stick into the burning fireplace as the little girl had often seen her parents do—but all Mrs. Jacobs could think about was that her children's lives had been spared. Although Mrs. Jacobs was not a Christian at this time and wanted little to do with spiritual matters, she had attended church as a girl and had enough religious upbringing to believe that God prompted her to return to the house.

———

Several years later, a second incident in Oma's childhood could have proven deadly. One afternoon little Oma played happily on the front porch, lost in childlike fantasy, wandering back and forth near a small wooden table. Finally tiring, Oma crawled up onto the porch swing. She wasn't there long when she saw the little table begin to shake. Suddenly, a rattlesnake slithered from under it and slid down the steps and out of sight. Even as a child, Oma understood God's protection over her.

———

An old family Bible records Oma Jacobs's birth: Dadeville, Alabama, October 18, 1895. In 1906, life on the

Jacobs's small farm was hard. Oma was the second of seven children. Her older sister, Monka, was never a strong child, so Oma helped her father with the farm chores in addition to assisting her mother in the house. The Jacobs children attended a little one-room country schoolhouse. Oma's early education consisted of basic lessons in penmanship, arithmetic, and reading. The students knew the rules even if they didn't always keep them: *At the end of class, wash your hands and face. Wash your feet if they are bare.*

On an ordinary day, Oma crawled out of bed at 4 a.m., completed her farm chores and household duties, and hurried off to school. She hated to miss, but each week on wash day, Oma stayed home from school to help her mother. Her job was to stir the family's laundry with a big stick as she walked around and around the huge, black pot heating water over an outside fire. Her best friend always helped her to catch up in her school lessons when Oma got behind.

Pray Expectantly

—

Out of the depths have I cried unto thee, O LORD. Lord, hear my voice: let thine ears be attentive to the voice of my supplications.

—Psalm 130:1–2

Message in the Cotton Field

Oma yanked at the fabric of her dress where it clung to her sweaty legs, and then she dragged her long pick-sack to the next row. As she rubbed her knees, she decided to give them a rest by bending over to pick the cotton bolls for a while instead of kneeling. The cotton had to be bright and clean or her father wouldn't get a good price, so she tossed aside the burrs and green bolls, careful not to get them in the large bag that hung across her shoulder. Each time her sack was full, she dragged it to the wagon and hung it on the scale to be weighed. While Oma was used to hard work, she labored especially hard when cotton-picking time rolled around. School was not going on at this time of year, and she was expected to do everything she could to help with the duties on the Jacobs's little farm.

The pickers had started as soon as the dew was off the cotton bolls on this day late in August. By now the sun beat down directly overhead, and Oma's throat felt as dry as the cotton between her slender fingers. Her feet were toughened from weeks of walking barefoot on the hot clay soil. She savored taking a dinner break to drink some refreshing water and eat a biscuit sandwich. Oma had packed food for herself and her father early this morning before they left for the field. She splashed some water on her face and then ladled some into her tin cup, gulped it down, and filled a cup for her father, who had just stepped up to the wagon along with the other pickers. "It looks like you've earned your keep this morning. Get some rest before starting on your next row," he told her as he took a drink of water.

Oma found a shady spot, tossed down her sack, and plopped right in the middle of it. She rubbed her fingers. No matter how hard she tried to avoid the little points, Oma always managed to come away with dry cracks and scratches from the sharp ends of the open cotton bolls. *I'm sure glad pickin' season is almost over*, she thought as she closed her eyes. Too soon her dinner break was over, and the pickers were back in the fields. Up one row and down the other, the tedious blanket of cotton seemed endless. But as Oma continued down another long row, something happened that made this afternoon different from all the rest. She heard the voice clearly, "Oma, give me your heart." The eleven-year-old girl had no doubt that it was the voice of the Lord.

Preachers took turns coming to the little Missionary Baptist Church that Oma attended regularly. Sometimes her own father served as a lay preacher in addition to his farming duties, so she heard the Bible taught many times. She even witnessed God's direct answer to her father's prayer when on one occasion the area experienced a bad drought. Her father prayed for rain while the other farmers mocked his efforts. God responded by sending a good rain to water the Jacobs's farm but passed right over the farms whose owners had scoffed at her father's prayers.

However, the incident in the cotton field that day confused her because their church taught that a child had to be twelve years old before accepting Christ and becoming a church member. So while Oma saw this call as real, she stood in the middle of the field that afternoon and, on the basis of her church's teaching, told God, "I can't give you my heart. I'm too young."

The Holy Spirit did not approach Oma again for a long time, and profound sadness marked the young girl's life through the following year. She had rejected the Lord, and the decision nagged at her. She understood that if she died, she would not go to heaven. Whenever she passed their rural cemetery, a frightening sense of death gripped her. Mrs. Jacobs noticed her daughter's increasing depression but was not aware of the reason behind it. Even if she had known, Mrs. Jacobs would not have understood why Oma felt such overwhelming sadness over her decision to hold off the call to salvation. Oma's mother was not aware that her daughter prayed in fear every day, "Lord, please don't let me die. Don't let me die!"

Mr. Jacobs, on the other hand, most likely saw Oma's need. He was a Christian, and although a stern and stoic individual by nature, he would have sensed she needed to be converted. That became evident to Oma when she came home one day and heard her father in prayer asking God for her salvation.

While it may be difficult to understand why Oma would have waited until she was twelve years old, when she was so confident God had talked to her audibly in the cotton field that day, she was naturally an obedient child, and she could not bring herself to disobey the laws of the church. The conflict that arose when she spent the next year in disobedience to God himself eventually became almost more than she could bear.

The following summer, Oma's church held a protracted meeting—what today is called a "revival." She was twelve years old by then, and as soon as the preacher brought the first day's meeting to a close, Oma ran down the aisle, ready to respond to the call of God and accept Jesus Christ as Savior before another minute passed. True to tradition in the small church, she readily gave a public testimony telling why she had come forward.

"Come now and be saved!" Oma pled boldly with any unsaved in the congregation. "Don't put it off!" She endured teasing from that day on because of the time "Oma Jacobs preached a sermon."

At the end of the meeting, Oma could not wait to get home and share the news with her mother. As was common, Mrs. Jacobs had not gone with her family to the church meeting. Oma charged into their farmhouse. "Mama, I got saved tonight. I'm going to heaven when I die!"

Oma's mother lifted the large apron she was wearing and flung it over her head, rejecting her daughter's startling news. The act was common in those days when houses were small, affording no place for privacy. Mrs. Jacobs's "retreat" sent an unmistakable message: "Let me be!"

Oma feared she had done wrong by speaking of salvation to her mother, so the young girl was surprised when, after a few minutes, Mrs. Jacobs lowered her apron. "I'm going to get saved. I want to go to heaven when I die, too." A few days after Oma accepted Christ, both her mother and her aunt attended the revival meeting and accepted Christ as Savior.

Many years later Mrs. Jacobs told her daughter, "I don't know if you've won anyone else to the Lord, but you sure won me." Oma wondered what prompted her mother to say such a thing because Oma knew her mother was saved at the church revival meeting—not the night Oma burst into their house and blurted out her glorious news. But Oma had forgotten that for a full year leading up to her conversion, she had been a very distraught girl. The night Oma rushed in with the joy of the Lord written all over her, Mrs. Jacobs witnessed the change that salvation had brought to her daughter. Oma now reflected the love of God, and her mother had witnessed the change. Given a few minutes to think it through, Mrs. Jacobs knew she wanted salvation for herself, too.

Pray with Assurance

—

Because he hath set his love upon me, therefore will I deliver him: I will set him on high, because he hath known my name. He shall call upon me, and I will answer him: I will be with him in trouble; I will deliver him, and honour him.

—Psalm 91:14–15

Remember the River

The day went routinely enough as their small congregation enjoyed a good church service and, later, dinner on the grounds. As they often did after a Sunday afternoon church dinner, Oma and some of the other young people decided to go rowing on the lake that opened out into the Tallapoosa River near Dadeville. The lake itself was usually calm, and from the group's vantage point, the Tallapoosa posed no threat.

"I'd keep off the river if I was you." An old man approached the young people headed for one of the boats at the dock. "We've had lots of stormy weather lately. Them's dangerous undercurrents!"

Oma Jacobs and her friends, all around sixteen years of age, ignored the man's warning and eagerly scrambled into the boat.

"Ya don't know what you're gettin' into," he yelled. "I'm tellin' ya, nobody oughta be goin' out today!"

The afternoon boat ride promised loads of fun, and the children rowed out onto the lake undaunted. No sooner had they begun to row than a strong current swept the little boat from the lake out into the middle of the Tallapoosa River. The exhilarated group took it as a challenge and rowed harder, but one by one, panic began to spread as they realized their strongest efforts weren't enough to control the direction of the boat.

"Let's get back to shore," one of them pleaded.

"Maybe that old man knew what he was talking about," another said fearfully.

"The water forms another lake down there," one of the kids pointed beyond the bend of the river. "Maybe things'll calm down then."

"Look! We're heading for the dam!" someone screamed.

In that dreadful moment, Oma imagined them being swept over the dam. They'd all be killed. "Do you need me, Lord?" Oma cried out. "Save me!" In an instant the boat landed safely on shore, and the children poured onto the safety of the dock. While there is no doubt that Oma was frightened for her life, her plea was much more than a cry for physical protection. *Lord, if you have something you want to do with my life, please save me so that I can serve you.* Putting the Lord first in her thoughts would prove to be a picture of Oma throughout her life.

The incident on the river resulted in an experience far different from what the group had planned. For Oma, it shaped her life profoundly, and she was never the same after it happened. "My life is yours forever, Lord," she vowed soon afterwards.

Oma's faith and her hunger for God's Word began to take firm root as the incident encouraged her to live a life of faith. She relayed the story often through the years, telling of the miracle God performed in that out-of-the-way place on a quiet Sunday afternoon in rural Alabama. "*Remember the river!*" she often said as, in spite of the passing years, the story remained vivid throughout her life.

The event on the river was not the first time God had intervened to protect Oma's life, but it would prove to be one of the most memorable. Oma's daughter, Elinor, said, "Mother never attempted to explain it, but she was sure of one thing—*God did it!*"

Pray with Thankfulness

Blessed be God, which hath not turned away my prayer, nor his mercy from me.

—Psalm 66:20

The Acquaintance

After completing high school, Oma attended Jacksonville Normal College in Alabama for two years. Finishing her college studies, she taught in country schools for the next seven years, sharing most of her earnings with her parents. Finally, when the seriousness of her family's financial situation became evident, Oma felt God's leading to take her savings and encourage everyone to move by train to Winter Garden, Florida, where working conditions were more favorable for her father. She enrolled in a bookkeeping course and worked for the next three years as a bookkeeper, along with caring for her parents' home because of her mother's ill health.

During her time in Winter Garden, Oma met a number of eligible men, but she didn't consider any of them in terms of marriage. Then one summer, a stranger played a role in changing that situation. Oma's church asked her to go to Deland, Florida, where the Southern Baptists were holding their annual Sunday School workshops on the campus of Stetson University.

An older gentleman seemed to appear at her every turn, asking her questions and making himself available to escort her to classes. Oma wondered about the man and why he took such an interest in her. She received her answer the day the gentleman showed up with a young man by his side. "I'd like you to meet my son, Martin Van Gelderen," he said. At that point, the man discreetly disappeared, giving his son freedom to take over.

The truth was now apparent to Oma. Martin's father had been out scouting for a good wife for his son. While Martin was shy, Oma was just the opposite, and Martin's father apparently believed that this woman and his son would create a good balance.

When the workshops were finished at the end of the week, Martin asked Oma for permission to write to her, and she eagerly consented. Their homes were just 250 miles apart, but in the early 1920s, that distance was considered much too far to run a Model-T Ford. The couple corresponded for a year. While they had not been able to spend much time getting to know each other during their initial acquaintance, they both believed that God had brought them together. The next summer Oma and Martin returned to the Sunday School workshops in Deland, Florida, eager to see each other again. While there, Martin made plans to spend a week with Oma's family. One night during that visit, as they sat on the front porch swing at her parents' home, he worked up the nerve to ask Oma to marry him. She happily consented.

Oma and Martin married the following January, and in 1924 they moved to Miami where Martin worked as a bookkeeper at the city hall. Her parents remained in Winter Garden. Martin Wayne (Wayne) was born in November, and the Van Gelderen family began to grow in size. Through various Christians God brought into her life, Oma also began to grow spiritually.

Pray Pleadingly

Hear my prayer, O LORD, and let my cry come unto thee.

—Psalm 102:1

The Promise

The "Great Miami Hurricane" devastated Miami, Florida, in September 1926. Winds as high as 125 miles per hour beat at the coastal city. Miamians had not experienced such damage in their lifetime, and there was little warning or preparation for the devastation. Broken windows, walls torn from their foundations, shortages of food—thousands experienced the losses. Many people died, and newspaper accounts estimated that up to 50,000 families lost their homes. Because of its economic impact, the violent storm helped usher the Great Depression into Florida sooner than in other areas of the country.

The Van Gelderens did not escape the devastation. High winds ripped off their neighbor's roof and crashed it onto Oma and Martin's house. At the height of the storm, Oma huddled in her small home, clutched her little boy in her arms, and cried out to God, "Lord, if you let us come out of this safely, I promise I will give you my whole life."

It was not the first time Oma had made such a bold commitment to God, and it was not the first time God had intervened in a crisis. When they surveyed the damage after the storm, she and Martin realized they had lost a large part of their belongings—including most of their wedding gifts. Those losses served Oma well the rest of her life. She shared with others throughout the years that this event helped to draw her attention closer to God. Material wealth in the form of money and everything it can buy held little interest for her. What could have been a very disheartening experience instead drew Oma nearer to the Lord. She witnessed firsthand how easily everything they owned could be wiped away in an instant. Oma grew spiritually as she began studying the Bible and eagerly going to hear the visiting preachers who came to Miami during the winter months. Except for a six-year period in her later years, Oma would spend the rest of her adult life serving the Lord in Florida.

Pray Diligently

—

Hear me, O LORD;
for thy lovingkindness
is good: turn unto
me according to
the multitude of thy
tender mercies.

—Psalm 69:16

The Message

Oma eventually began teaching a Sunday School class for children. Then the day came when one of the church women asked Oma to give a devotion at their Women's Missionary Union monthly meeting. Oma had never taught adults and had no idea what to talk about. "I only teach children," Oma responded emphatically. In her mind, that was the end of it. The woman, however, did not take her response seriously. "I'll count on you to do it," she said confidently.

During the next month, Oma read and studied fervently. She had no idea how to prepare a talk, and as the deadline drew near, she had made little progress. She had not been given guidelines concerning the subject matter, so she began to search through the biblical materials she had in her home, but that search did not bring the results she had hoped. Time was drawing to a close, and still she had no idea what God wanted her to do. The night before the meeting, Oma crawled into bed and poured her heart out. "Lord, I'm disappointed. You haven't given me a talk. I'm going to disgrace your name tomorrow because I'm not ready." At that moment the Holy Spirit began to communicate with her. "Wait a minute, Lord," Oma said. "Let me get a pencil and paper."

Oma made her way down the hall and to the kitchen where she sat down at the table. "All right, Lord, now I'm ready." The Holy Spirit directed her, and soon she had a message based on 1 Corinthians 15:58, "Therefore my beloved brethren, be ye stedfast, unmoveable, always abounding in the work of the Lord, forasmuch as ye know that your labour is not in vain in the Lord." When the Holy Spirit stopped communicating, Oma knew the work was accomplished, and she returned to bed with a settled heart.

The following morning Oma dressed for the meeting, gathered her Bible and notes, and started out on the walk to the church. But she didn't like the looks of the sky and very soon felt the first drops of rain. Once again Oma approached God confidently. "Lord, I have to give your talk this morning. Surely you don't want me to get wet! I need you to stop the rain until I get to church. And, please, I need one more thing, Lord. I need the janitor to be in the entryway when I get there, so he can go up to my third-floor Sunday School room and get my flannel-graph board."

Oma didn't make demands on God because she felt some special right to do so. She simply figured that God had given her the devotional message, and she could go to him to carry out the remaining details, too. She continued down the sidewalk confident of God's control of the situation.

Oma had barely stepped inside when the downpour broke loose. Not only that, God had old Ben, the janitor, waiting in the foyer. "If there's anything you need, I'd be glad to help," he offered.

"Would you please go up to my Sunday School room and bring me my flannel-graph board?" she asked kindly. Then she breathed a prayer of gratitude to God for his provisions.

Women attending the meeting complimented Oma after her talk.

"You gave a wonderful message."

"What a blessing."

"That was just what I needed to hear."

Oma responded to each comment without hesitation. "You can thank the Lord. It was *his* talk." Only Oma knew how literally true that was. And although she continued to speak periodically throughout the years, God never again gave her a message in quite that same way. "He didn't need to," she said. "He taught me how."

Pray Dependently

—

Hear my prayer, O God;
give ear to the words
of my mouth.
—Psalm 54:2

The Jonah Fleece

When Oma and Martin's son Wayne was a young man, Oma experienced a growing awareness that God was going to call him to preach, but it made little sense because Wayne was extremely shy, and he stuttered severely—barely able to put two words together without slips. Oma kept to herself her belief that God would ultimately call her son into ministry. She knew that fourteen-year-old Wayne wanted to be an engineer. He had no desire whatsoever to become a preacher. While she did not try to persuade her son otherwise, Oma began to pray in earnest.

Soon Oma saw the evidences of the Lord's work in changing Wayne's heart. The day came when Wayne surrendered his life to full-time Christian service, wondering at the time if God was calling him to preach but reasoning that with his stuttering problem that surely couldn't be. In fact, when Wayne answered an altar call and shared that he thought he had been called to preach, his pastor hesitated. He knew the boy had no outward signs that he could handle the task. "Son, not everybody has to preach in order to serve God," he said kindly.

Yet Wayne couldn't shake the feeling that this was exactly what God wanted him to do, and he shared it with his mother. Of course, it was no surprise to her, but to confirm it in Wayne's heart, she suggested they put out the fleece. Up until that time, Oma had not confided in Wayne that she had been asking God for this very thing to happen. Now she made a suggestion. "We're going to choose three good churches in the city and attend each one of them. If all three sermons are on Bible passages concerning Jonah, we'll know God has spoken and intends for you to enter the ministry."

The pastor of the first church they visited preached on Jonah. The pastor of the second church they visited preached on Jonah. Then they attended the third church. When the preacher got up to speak that morning, he announced that he had planned to preach on a different topic, but the Holy Spirit had changed the preacher's mind and impressed upon him to preach the story of Jonah!

Wayne and his mother exchanged knowing glances. Years later when Wayne studied the biblical passage concerning Gideon, he came to the understanding that they were wrong to have put out a fleece in the manner they had done, but still God had honored the request—perhaps because it was asked in innocence. Wayne was a young man who stuttered greatly. If he were to preach God's Word, he needed a resounding reassurance that God would be there alongside him. God chose to answer the request that he must have deemed Wayne had made in sincere ignorance. After God confirmed Wayne's call to preach through the Jonah sermons, in faith Wayne entered a sermon contest that involved preacher boys in the southern half of Florida. Apparently, God loosed his tongue because he was awarded second place!

Pray Earnestly

—

Let my prayer be set forth before thee as incense; and the lifting up of my hands as the evening sacrifice.

—Psalm 141:2

The Choice

When the time came to choose a college, Wayne made the decision to go to Bob Jones University. During his college years, Oma faithfully interceded for him in prayer. On one occasion her son talked to her about a certain woman for whom he had a growing fondness, but he shared with his mother that the woman was trying to persuade him to go into the field of education instead of the preaching ministry. Oma prayed fervently that God would settle this matter, and in God's timing, the relationship ended. As time went on, Wayne became seriously interested in another college acquaintance. This time his brother, Bobby, alerted their mother to the situation. Bobby was concerned because, once again, a woman was discouraging Wayne from going into the pastorate and, instead, encouraging him to settle for the field of education.

Oma's concern was not because she wanted her own way. If her son had felt God's call to teach, then she would have rejoiced in that call. Her concern was because her son was confident that God had called him to preach, and she saw these two separate incidents in Wayne's life as having the potential to draw him away from God's will. She prayed fervently that her son would find a mate who was in agreement with what God wanted to do in his life. Oma watched as the Lord closed the door to both of these marriage prospects. Wayne acknowledged many times over the ensuing years that his mother "prayed him out of those relationships," and he was extremely thankful to her and to God.

After Wayne graduated from BJU, he took a small Baptist church to pastor. Mrs. F. H. McDonald, an influential woman in the convention and his mother's close spiritual mentor, knew of a little church in Miami that needed a pastor, and she suggested it to Wayne. The church leaders weren't enthusiastic about hiring a young man right out of college; however, Wayne answered all of the deacons' questions to their satisfaction, so they called him to be their new pastor at Sylvania Heights Baptist Church.

Wayne saw results immediately. He was a warm, mild-mannered preacher of substance, not at all animated, yet people were often glued to his preaching. That in itself was God's doing. When Wayne had been in college, he had received speech training, and over time, God had taken his stuttering problem away completely. The Lord's presence was evident in his messages, and the Holy Spirit filled him as he spoke. The church grew under Wayne's leadership, doubling in size several times before God called him to a new church. Many of the people in his congregation were new converts. God's hand was unmistakably on his ministry at Sylvania Heights. All the while, he was aware that his mother prayed quietly and fervently in the background and that God honored her "effectual, fervent prayers."

When he had been a pastor for about five years, Wayne was invited by a preacher friend to come and hold a three-week revival meeting in the preacher's church in Chicago. Since the preacher was not going to be there at the time, he asked Wayne if he would mind having a certain young lady show him around the city. Wayne and the young woman, Tirrell, hit it off, and it soon became apparent they were headed into a serious relationship.

Some time later, Wayne received a second invitation to speak at a revival in Chicago. This time Tirrell invited Wayne to meet her brother who lived in Maroa, Illinois. After that meeting, Wayne issued an invitation to Tirrell to come down to Miami for Thanksgiving to meet his family. Oma and Martin liked Tirrell, and it quickly became apparent that this was the woman God had chosen for Wayne—the wife Oma had prayed God would bring into her son's life.

Tirrell was an orphan, but she had some godly cousins who had influenced her. Although she lived in a horrible situation and had no parents to guide her, Tirrell's life was clean from the wickedness around her. Wayne knew that his mother had prayed in earnest for the woman he would one day marry and that the Lord had kept his hand on her life even as a young girl.

It was during the Thanksgiving visit that Wayne asked Tirrell to marry him. He gave her an engagement ring, and they made plans for their wedding. Tirrell came to love her mother-in-law deeply, and Oma returned that love. Their relationship was to remain free of tension and struggles throughout their lives.

Pray in Season

—

My voice shalt thou hear
in the morning, O LORD;
in the morning will I direct
my prayer unto thee,
and will look up.

—Psalm 5:3

Trying Times

A few years before Wayne and Tirrell were wed, Oma's second son, Bobby, had met and married a woman named Barbara. About two years into Bobby and Barbara's marriage, they were in a serious auto accident. Dr. John R. Rice had asked Bobby to join the Rice Ministry, and it happened as Bobby and Barbara were on their way home from meeting with Dr. Rice in Wheaton, Illinois. The accident left both Bobby and Barbara with critical injuries.

At that same time, Wayne's wife, Tirrell, had a tubal pregnancy, and the doctor was concerned about her life. To add to the trials, Oma received news that her mother had terminal cancer, and death was imminent. Oma had to take a bus between the two hospitals where her daughters-in-law were patients. They were at death's door; her son was injured permanently, and her mother was nearing her last days. One day, as she sat on a bus stop bench with tears flowing down her cheeks, Oma reminded the Lord of 1 Corinthians 10:13: "There hath no temptation taken you but such as is common to man: but God is faithful, who will not suffer you to be tempted above that ye are able; but will with the temptation also make a way to escape, that ye may be able to bear it." She laid it all out to the Lord, pleading that it was time for him to intercede and help her.

Oma's mother lived 250 miles away. Oma desperately wanted to be there for her mother's funeral when the time came, but her son and both sons' wives were in critical condition. She did not feel she could leave under the circumstances and again turned to God to intervene. Jeremiah 32:17 sustained Oma through these trying days: "Ah Lord GOD! behold, thou hast made the heaven and the earth by thy great power and stretched out arm, and there is nothing too hard for thee . . ." Within a few short days, the Lord brought her mother out of a coma long enough for both daughters-in-law to improve. By the time God chose to take her mother home to heaven, Oma confidently felt she could leave her family to attend the funeral. The Lord interceded and delayed her mother's home-going, and the trial strengthened Oma's faith. Oma hadn't just believed God *could* answer her plea; she had believed he *would* answer it.

Eventually both Tirrell and Barbara were restored to good health. But the auto accident left twenty-two-year-old Bobby a paraplegic. He spent five months in the hospital, after which he lived with his parents and sister, Elinor, for a year of recuperation. Eventually he and Barbara were able to return to their own home where they lived until Barbara's death nearly thirty years later.

Pray Out of Season

—

Then they cry unto the LORD in their trouble, and he bringeth them out of their distresses.

—Psalm 107:28

The Convincement

On one occasion, Wayne had been pastoring a church in Detroit, Michigan, for several years. His mother, who was now a widow, came up from Florida to visit her son and his family. One evening he had a speaking engagement at an out-of-town church. While Wayne was preaching, a snow storm began brewing outside. At the conclusion of the meeting, as he prepared for the long drive home, he realized that the storm was much worse than he had anticipated. However, he had an important speaking engagement the next morning close to home, and he felt he had no choice but to try to make it back that night.

Wayne called his wife, Tirrell. "We're in the midst of a full-blown blizzard. People here are saying it looks worse than anything they've seen in a long time. The weather is bad—ice on the road, heavy winds, and blowing snow." He asked his wife to pray and to share the need with his mother.

The storm forced cars into ditches all along the route. Wayne worked his way through the blinding snow, barely able to see where he was going. Suddenly, he saw something glittering off to the side of the road. He wasn't sure what it was, but he decided to keep going. Instantly, he felt a compelling urgency to stop and investigate and immediately saw that the "glitter" was a railroad crossing light covered with ice except for a tiny slice of light breaking through. Almost at the same moment, a speeding train crossed immediately in front of his vehicle. The preacher was overwhelmed with the realization of what would have happened if he had not sensed the strong compulsion to stop his car.

At the breakfast table the next morning, Wayne told his family about his remarkable experience at the railroad tracks the night before. He was overwhelmed with the sense that the Holy Spirit had constrained him to stop and investigate instead of proceeding on as he had first planned.

Wayne had known his mother would be concerned. She was not experienced with winter blizzards, having spent most of her life in the more tropical climate of Florida, so he never doubted that she would take the dangerous weather conditions he was facing seriously. But he was even more overcome with the knowledge of God's protective hand when his mother shared how God had worked in her heart the previous evening.

"Mom went to the Scriptures, just as she was in the habit of doing when getting ready to pray," Wayne said. "She was afraid for me, and that took her to God's Word as she sought wisdom in how she should pray." She said she continued praying and reading Scriptures late into the evening—refusing to give up until the Lord had given her faith. When finally she came to 2 Peter 2:9, "The Lord knoweth how to deliver the godly out of temptations," the Holy Spirit flooded her with a settled peace. God gave her confirmation that he had heard her prayer for me. She laid her Bible down, crawled into bed, and fell sound asleep."

Many years later, shortly before Wayne died, he was reminiscing with his sister, Elinor, about that night so long ago. "It's still very vivid in my mind," he told her. "I could not see that fast moving train. I had no doubt then, and I have no doubt to this day that the Holy Spirit impressed me to stop. If I had not heeded the warning, I would have been killed."

Pray Patiently

—

But unto thee have I cried, O LORD; and in the morning shall my prayer prevent thee.

—Psalm 88:13

To the Third Generation

When Oma's grandchildren came along, she started praying for each of them earnestly. John, the youngest grandson, was born on the western slope of the Rocky Mountains in the little town of Durango in the southwest corner of Colorado, but his family moved from there to Chicago when he was just four years old. He doesn't remember a lot about Colorado, but his oldest brother, Wayne Jr., who was twelve at the time, was aware of what a big change this move brought. The family went from cowboy boots and horses to the South Side of Chicago where their father, Wayne, had taken a new church.

The youth group at their new church was not in a healthy condition. In fact, it was full of worldliness—a drawing away from God and a growing acceptance of sinful choices. Wayne Jr.'s mom and dad became increasingly burdened about their oldest son. He was choosing friends that had no interest in godly living, and he himself displayed a lack of interest in the things of the Lord. They observed a growing disinterest in the teachings of the Bible and a growing interest in unwise friendships and direction. While he was not in serious trouble yet, his parents sensed it was close at hand. One day, that concern caused Wayne to call his mother in Florida to ask her to pray earnestly for her grandson.

After their phone conversation, Oma went to her Bible to seek the Lord's direction. She knew her fifteen-year-old grandson was in the habit of throwing himself fully into his activities. He had been involved in both band and sports in the public high school he attended, but when he developed a heart murmur due to a rapid growth spurt, the doctor had instructed the young man to curtail his sports activities. Oma knew that might have caused him some discouragement.

One day Oma called in response to her earlier conversation with her son about Wayne Jr. At that time, her son was getting ready to take a group of his church people on a trip to the Holy Land. "God has heard," she told her son joyfully. "Wayne Jr. is going with you on that Bible Lands trip, and God is going to use it to change his life." While his mother was rejoicing in the Lord on her end of the phone, her son Wayne sounded skeptical on the other end.

"Mom, I appreciate that, but it is impossible for Wayne Jr. to go on the trip. There are no seats available on the plane, and even if there were, I wouldn't have the money to pay for the ticket. In addition, it's too late to get the passport and visa."

"Son, you don't understand." His mother was not to be swayed. "God has borne witness with my spirit. I'm telling you, Wayne Jr. is going, and God is going to use it to change his life." She then proceeded to clap her hands to the Lord like only she could do.

At that point, her son backed off. He knew from long experience that when his mother reached this point in her praying, it was completed. It was going to happen!

Days before the departure for Israel, a deacon in the church who had planned to go on the trip was forced to back out because of family health problems. Since it was too late for a refund, the deacon asked Pastor Van Gelderen to give the ticket to someone else.

The preacher was overwhelmed. He knew immediately it was God's way of providing. He drove to the high school to pick up his son. They went into Chicago to get the passport and visa for Wayne Jr. and persuaded the authorities to issue the documents on the spot. The next day, with his passport and visa in hand, Wayne Jr. was officially among the group going to Israel. It had all happened so fast that the boy was in a whirlwind at the beginning of the trip. His aunt Elinor was among the group, and she said he sat alone at the back of the bus for most of the tour. "My brother talked about the various sites as we visited them," said Aunt Elinor. I recall vividly as one by one we entered the Garden Tomb. I was with my nephew when he stepped inside. I remember watching him turn and gaze at the empty slab. As he turned back around, tears were streaming down his cheeks. We did not know what was going on in his heart at the time, but it was evident from his reaction that something significant was taking place."

The first Sunday back home, Wayne Jr. made his feelings public. During the invitation at the end of the church service, he burst down the aisle and threw his arms around his father. "I want to surrender my life to full-time Christian service," he cried. "If Jesus was willing to do what he did for me, then I should be willing to serve God and give my life fully to him."

"My nephew was saved at four years old and has held to that confidence throughout his life," said his Aunt Elinor. "But the reality of what the Lord had done for him became real at the Garden Tomb. The decision he made when he returned home from Israel was a direct result of that realization."

Neither Wayne Jr.'s father nor his aunt knew just how much the events of the trip had affected the teenager, until he shared it with his family upon his return home. He told about the personal spiritual struggle that warred within him during this trip. He felt the Lord working on his heart and had time to try to put the pieces of his life together and to sum up what Christ had done for him.

"When we reached the Garden Tomb and were in a preaching session, the Spirit of God stirred Wayne Jr.'s heart in a deep and very personal way," said Aunt Elinor. "He said he awoke to the reality of who Christ is, that he actually rose again, and that he is alive and working. Those truths began to bear down in the heart of my nephew."

Wayne Jr.'s decision sparked a spiritual revival in his entire church youth group. One by one the kids caught on fire for the Lord. Because the teenagers attended various schools all over the South Side of Chicago, the church's youth pastor visited different public schools each day for lunch—holding prayer meetings and seeing young people saved. Wayne Jr.'s youngest brother, John, remembers it as a little boy. "I would hear the teenagers in my dad's church talk about Jesus—being thrilled with who Jesus was and seeing this kid saved and praying for that kid. And I remember thinking, 'I can hardly wait to become a teenager so I can talk like that!'"

There are men preaching the Gospel today who came out of that youth group. In later years, John and the middle brother, Jim, would both turn the direction of their lives to service for the Lord. Their decisions were directly influenced by the youth revival that took place during this time. Again, their grandma had heard the need, sought God's will from his Word, and then claimed that will in faith. God gave the increase in faith.

Pray with Sincerity

—

I cried unto the LORD with my voice; with my voice unto the LORD did I make my supplication.

—Psalm 142:1

Mother Van: How She Prayed

With every year that passed, Oma seemed to gain a clearer understanding of going to God with his own words. As she began her reading, the Word increased her faith. When someone called her with a special prayer request, she didn't begin to pray immediately. She went to the Scriptures first and read until faith welled within her. It was only then that she knew what request to bring before the Lord. God's Word became an inseparable part of her intercession. It wasn't just about praying God's promises. It was about first going to his Word and seeking his will in a given situation. Once Oma understood how God was directing her to pray on a given matter, it was as good as settled because it was his request, not her own. If she had a special burden, she read the Scriptures that applied to the need, and once she began she didn't give up until the Holy Spirit gave her the assurance that God had spoken. Hers was a simple faith that whatever God promised, he was faithful to complete.

While in the early years of her prayer life, there may have been times when Oma wrongly interpreted her own strong desires as the Holy Spirit's conviction. As she matured spiritually, she grew to recognize the difference between her own desires and God's will. It is not known at exactly what point Oma came to this step in her spiritual growth, but eventually she learned how to effectively pray the will of God revealed through scriptural promises. That is the key to how she became such a vital prayer warrior.

Oma prayed for personal requests across America and around the world. She prayed for family members, church members, and friends of church members. She prayed for missionaries. She even prayed for a prominent baseball player who had spiritual needs. Word about her intercessory prayer ministry spread far and wide.

In her later years, during the time her prayer ministry was most active, Oma came to be known as "Mother Van."

On one particular occasion, a missionary who had heard about "Mother Van" from a pastor he knew called her with an urgent prayer request. An acquaintance of the missionary had contracted leprosy. At that time leprosy was a death sentence. The missionary asked Oma to pray that God heal the leper. She immediately began searching the Scriptures for God's direction in the matter. Was he directing her to pray for healing or something else? Once she was confident God had given her the scriptural passage to seek divine healing, she appealed to the Great Physician. The missionary later reported that God miraculously removed the "incurable" disease from the leper.

"There are so many accounts of divine intervention as a result of Grandma's prayers—some of them so remarkable that if I weren't related to her, I'd wonder about the truth of them," Oma's grandson John admits. "The fact is, Grandma had glorious, remarkable answers to prayer."

"Grandma's prayers were always accompanied with tears," middle grandson Jim remembers. "I don't ever recall seeing her pray that she didn't cry. She could cry and pray and talk at the same time. Her habit of sitting down and crying and sharing Scripture often scared me as a child. Somehow I seemed to be laid bare when I was with her. I guess I knew that she had it and that I didn't! When she prayed, those around her could depend upon her getting the ear of God. She seemed to be in a dimension they knew nothing about. The interesting thing is that Grandma was a woman not easily brought to tears. She had experienced a hard upbringing, and she rarely shed a tear—except when she prayed—and she always cried when she prayed."

One time John asked Aunt Elinor about this. "When people called Grandma and asked her to pray, I know she prayed, but just how did she go about it?" Aunt Elinor said that John's grandma would take her well-worn Bible, sit down on her favorite place on the sofa, and begin to talk to God as if he were there with her in the room. There was nothing magical about that sofa. It was just a place she often went to when she began to pray. She knew the Lord, and she talked to him in a very personal way that went something like this: "Now God, here's a need. God, I know you can meet the need, but I don't know if you will. Now God, what is your will here?"

Aunt Elinor told John that his grandma might search a Scripture passage where the Spirit of God had spoken to her before to see if God would give life there again. Sometimes God would, and sometimes he would guide her to another passage, but Oma understood she had to have the will of God based on the Word of God before she could pray with confidence.

Oma had the habit of reading all of the promises God had spoken to her in the past, reading them again until he spoke to her through those verses again, and then confidently claiming them. She did not use prayer as a tactic to manipulate circumstances or make claims on God outside of his will. Only when she was confident God had spoken to her would she know the concern was going to be worked out.

Oma had many experiences in which God spoke to her through the voice of the Holy Spirit. She knew more than anyone else knew that it was God who performed the work. She was only a weak vessel in the hands of the Master Potter. On the other hand, she was not shy in proclaiming her confidence in God once he confirmed his answer within her. As explained in "Three Connected Truths Concerning Prayer" included in this book, at that point in Oma's prayer she would cry out, "I've got it!" What Oma meant she had was the ear of God—the completion of the specific prayer she had brought before God's throne. Those who witnessed her do this knew she wasn't making light of the situation or boasting. She was merely proclaiming the truth that God had answered and would manifest that answer in his appointed time. At that point, Oma knew she need not pray any longer about the matter. Like a letter that has been dropped into the mail slot at the post office, the answer to the prayer was now on its way. The difference is that when God sends a message, it is guaranteed to be delivered!

Did "Mother Van" have a special connection to God? Yes, she did. However, any Christian who surrenders 100 percent to God also has that special connection. God became everything to Oma, and that resulted in her walking in the fullness of the power of the Holy Spirit. That power is available to all Christians who are completely surrendered to God.

Pray Consistently

—

Evening, and morning, and at noon, will I pray, and cry aloud: and he shall hear my voice.

—Psalm 55:17

The Woman They Knew

"My dad's brother and his wife lived next door throughout my brothers' and my growing up years," said Elinor. "Mother loved to plant flowers. Sometimes her freshly planted flowers would disappear. Mother soon figured out that my aunt had transplanted those missing flowers into her own yard. This happened many times. Over the years I watched my mother practice the scriptural directive of overcoming evil with good as she took my aunt a fresh-baked pie or some homemade bread," Elinor remembers. "Through it all, my aunt declared one day that Mother must be an angel!"

In later years, Elinor and her mother lived in Miami next door to an eccentric woman who was always angry with them. As was Oma's habit, she returned the anger with kindness, usually in the form of something she had baked. Eventually the neighbor woman developed cancer, and she spread the word to the neighbors: "You'd better not say anything bad about Mrs. Van or something will happen to you." While bringing harm to this woman was certainly not Oma's motive or desire, apparently her kindness had stirred the neighbor woman's conscience.

———

The Lord meant more to Oma than anything else. While she worked hard and looked after her family well, if Jesus had come to her door, she would have been like Mary in the New Testament. She would have stopped what she was doing and gone to kneel before the feet of Jesus, remaining there to soak in everything he had to say. "I have been privileged to know many people who love the Lord and serve him in sincerity, but I have only met one other woman in my entire life whose prayer ministry compared to Grandma's," said grandson Jim.

"Grandma prayed my father into the ministry. I have no doubt that she also prayed all three of us grandsons into the ministry," said Jim. "When she prayed, miracles happened; there is no doubt! We constantly witnessed answers to prayer in our family. Her conversations with God were real. The fact that there are so many members of her extended family in full-time ministry is no accident."

"Grandma had a joyful outlook on life, but Grandpa Van Gelderen wasn't as easily amused as Grandma," said Jim. "Grandpa went through the Great Miami Hurricane, the Great Depression, and the Florida Land Bust. He and Grandma lost what land they had, and it left him negative and disappointed. Grandma went through those same things, but she handled them differently—even the little irritations of life didn't get to her like they do most people. If they had a flat tire, Grandpa grumbled and Grandma laughed. The more she laughed, the madder Grandpa got." Jim chuckled. "It wasn't that Grandma was making fun of Grandpa, for she loved him very much. It was just that she found delight, and even sometimes amusement, in things that were beyond her control."

"Grandpa's children loved him dearly, and they respected him. He was a good father and a good grandfather. However, he missed the joy of the Lord that Grandma possessed. Yet, while Grandma was the stronger spiritual influence in their home, I can't say that she *ran* the house. She was wise and kept a good balance in that respect," said Jim. "I always felt that Grandma was content with her place and felt no need to struggle for power or control."

Oma never had a lot of money. She was brought up without much in the way of material belongings, and while some might have reacted adversely to that upbringing, she found it easy to do without. During the years of the Great Depression, Martin and Oma saw that their children had food on the table and clothes to wear, but it was only after they were grown that the Van Gelderen children realized they had been quite poor. Their mother just didn't emphasize it. She consistently had a song in her heart—singing or humming much of the time. Her children remember hearing her hum as she worked outside. The contentment she exemplified gave them the security that they need not worry about anything, and they knew if they asked their mother to pray for them, she would do it. She loved the Lord deeply, and that love overflowed to those who came in contact with her.

The stout, jovial woman also had a great laugh, and she knew how to enjoy life. Jim recalled an example of how she was able to take in stride what could have been considered an embarrassing disaster. "Grandma was famous for her macaroni and cheese. One time the family gathered around the table, and since Grandma just happened to be serving macaroni and cheese, it reminded her of an amusing story, and she began to share it with us," remembers Jim. "'One night we had the neighbors over for supper,' Grandma began to chuckle as she told on herself.

'When we sat down to eat, I realized I had left the *macaroni* out of the macaroni and cheese!'"

"We all had a good laugh at Grandma's story," said Jim, "but the funniest part came when one by one we realized that Grandma had left the macaroni out of *our* macaroni and cheese that night, too! I remember her putting her hand to her mouth so her false teeth wouldn't fall out. She got so tickled that I thought she'd never stop laughing—but that was Grandma," Jim recalls fondly.

"Grandma had a serious side, though. She was a phenomenal disciplinarian and would go through an unbelievable ordeal—weeping as she considered and prayed over how to handle a behavior problem with one of her children. She'd spank, and they'd cry. She'd spank again, and they'd cry some more," said Jim. "She had a strong constitution and firm convictions; yet even in this, she exemplified a joy through it all. Grandma used the belt on the two boys and switches on her daughter. She always referred to Scriptures when talking with them, but she didn't use the Bible as a whip when disciplining. She used it to teach principles. She was very firm with the grandchildren, too."

"Grandma was a great storyteller, too. My aunt Elinor has said that when my father, Wayne, or my mother, Tirrell, would call and share a problem they were facing with one of us children, Grandma would frame those character issues into stories. She did that even when her own three children were young. Her Aunt Molly stories were for Aunt Elinor when she was a girl. Occasionally she'd tell a single story, but more often than not it was from a series she had put together," said Jim. "The Aunt Molly stories and a series about a bear were two that she used in particular. 'I have something I want to share with you,' Grandma would begin. And she always slipped in a moral lesson along the way. Whenever Grandma planned a trip to Colorado where my family lived at one time, she would find out what problems we children were facing, and then she would weave a story for each of us," said Jim. "Unfortunately, as with many good stories, no one thought at the time to put them in writing."

"I believe God called Grandma specifically to the work of intercessory prayer," said Jim. From his earliest memories in the 1960s, his grandma was a spiritual dynamic—a happy Christian—one who often clapped her hands when she talked about the Lord. "She didn't come from an ideal situation. Her older sister, Monka, was their mother's favorite, and Grandma carried a heavy workload as a young girl. Though my grandpa, Martin, never grasped the victorious aspect of the Christian life, Grandma kept a vision," said Jim.

Oma prayed fervently for her children, Wayne, Bobby, and Elinor, and her grandchildren, Wayne Jr., Joy, Jim,

John, and Joanna. Her grandsons are in full-time ministry as pastors or evangelists, and her two granddaughters married pastors. All have remained faithful in the Lord's service. "None of that happened by mistake," said Jim.

In addition to this, Oma's daughter, Elinor, served the Lord faithfully in the field of education and eventually went on to teach at the Baptist College of Ministry in Menomonee Falls, Wisconsin. Oma's son Bobby, although left a paraplegic after his severe auto accident, spent his life in the Christian counseling ministry, which took him all over America. Several years after his wife Barbara's death, Bobby met and married Rosemary, who cared for him devotedly for the rest of his life.

Oma had no Bible college training, but her theological knowledge could be matched against some of the finest Bible scholars. She grew to know her Bible because she lived in it daily. Mrs. F. H. McDonald, who had led Martin to the Lord before he married Oma, became the young wife's mentor after the marriage. Mrs. McDonald took a loving interest in Oma, holding many Bible lessons and giving counseling sessions over the telephone. Oma attended Mrs. McDonald's Sunday School class until beginning to teach classes herself. An avid learner, Oma was eager to know more and more of the Word of God. She went to hear preachers whenever the opportunity arose, and she invited many into the Van Gelderen home as guests.

Oma never knew a stranger, as she considered everyone a neighbor. She was marked by a selfless countenance, and she was always witnessing the truth of the Gospel to those with whom she came in contact. She was outgoing, so speaking of her beloved Lord was not difficult for her. When a person had an urgent need, she would stop any activity to pray. Yet, although prayer time was natural for Oma, she showed a humble side and tried to get out of leading the prayer when asked in a family setting. She did not want to put her prayers out in front of anyone else. Though she had a very unusual prayer ministry and one that people may today consider mystical or strange, she was not considered odd by most of her friends. People were deeply and warmly touched by her. She exemplified such a joy that they had no desire to be critical.

Dr. Al C. Janney was Oma's pastor for a while in Florida. By the time he met Oma, her seventy-nine years had stooped her figure, and rheumatism had slowed her walk. Dr. Janney remembers her well. "She didn't spend a lot of time talking about her health or her personal needs. She was a sweet woman with a very positive outlook—marked by a sense of humility. It seemed she was always smiling."

"Even before she came to our church, we already knew of her reputation as a woman who got her prayers answered," said Dr. Janney. "When there was a serious prayer request, someone would suggest we call Mother Van."

Oma's long-time friend and prayer partner, Gloria Cain, also spoke warmly of dear Mother Van and the many hours they spent praying together over the needs of others. "I have never been sure whether Mother Van crossed my life or if it was the other way around. Our relationship was God's gift to each of us. It was immediate at our meeting and was certainly God-centered. I had asked God for a seasoned prayer partner as I was a teacher and concerned for souls. He gave me a great lady of faith, a faithful warrior, and sister in Christ," Gloria said. "We both communicated with our Lord, prayed without ceasing—in an attitude of worship always; our relationship together was as two or more gathered in his name; we saw heaven come down and glory filled our souls for sure."

"Oma was quite funny," said Gloria. "She had such a quirky sense of humor. One day she said, 'I just have to get Elinor to take me to get my hair cut and washed. My head looks like a bug under a cabbage!' Then she would laugh with that great chuckle-y laugh she had. Sometimes I would drive over and take her to a Swedish restaurant we both liked. 'Come on, Gloria, let's dig in.' she'd say once they brought out the food."

Even though there was a vast difference in their ages, Oma and Gloria were prayer partners for ten years and close friends much longer. "Oma had her own unique way of talking about God," Gloria said. She would tell how she was concerned about such and such a thing. Then she would say, 'I talked it over with the Lord, and he told me that it was okay. He's taken care of my account!' Then she would be fine about the particular concern," Gloria remembers. "When faith came to Mother Van, she didn't take it back. When someone disturbed her peace with an offence or interruption of some kind, she would say, 'I mean to get along!' While she had needs that shook and tried her at times just like everyone else, she exemplified a personal relationship with her Father and rested upon that foundation."

Gloria added, "Oma knew she was chosen, not because of her ability but because of God's power. She was loved and trusted by many as a gracious and powerful prayer warrior. Indeed, *her works have followed her.* Mother Van could pray at the drop of a hat with anyone of God's very own. She was a preacher's warrior and a true mentor to all.

"Anytime Mother Van had a need herself, she would get on the phone and call people to see if someone else needed prayer. 'If I take care of his business, he will take care of mine,' she would say. Even when things did not go as she had wished, Mother Van 'had a mind to get along.' She lived Acts 24:16, 'And herein do I exercise myself, to have always a conscience void to offence toward God, and toward men.'"

Pray in Faith

The LORD is nigh unto all them that call upon him, to all that call upon him in truth.

—Psalm 145:18

She Still Knew How to Pray

In the late 1980s, Oma's grandson Jim had been married only a few years when he and his wife, Rhonda, began to long for a child. They prayed but saw no results. Jim had not seen his grandma for quite some time and looked forward to spending some time with her. He also wanted very much to share the desire for a child with his grandma. The effectiveness of her prayers was something that would live in his memory. He and Rhonda decided to make a trip to Florida.

When Jim called Uncle Bobby to make arrangements to go and visit Grandma, Uncle Bobby warned him to be prepared for a drastic change in her.

"She is no longer the woman you remember," said Uncle Bobby.

"I'd still like to see her," said Jim. But Jim wasn't prepared for his grandma's frail condition. In addition to the physical losses, she had lost her memory and, for the first time, did not know her grandson. "I was shocked and saddened by her decline, yet in all of this, one thing hadn't changed. Uncle Bobby told us that Grandma still prayed and was still able to reach God with her prayers."

Jim and Rhonda made an attempt to explain their prayer request to Jim's grandma. "Would you please pray that God will give us a child?" he asked carefully.

"We struggled to get her to comprehend. It was heartbreaking, but it was apparent to us that age had taken its toll on Grandma." Then, just as they had come to the conclusion that their appeal had fallen on deaf ears, Jim's grandma began to pray. While Jim doesn't remember the words of her prayer, he does remember how she looked when she was finished. "'*You've got it,*' she said. That was the grandma I remembered! She never said that unless she *knew* God had answered!"

From that point on, Jim was confident God would give them a child. Jim had witnessed his grandma's prayers too many times to count, and he knew that her request had been heard. "Somewhere along the line I came to peace that we would have at least one child—even though the answer did not come for another six or seven years with some miscarriages in between. I was very familiar with my grandma's walk with the Lord. I had learned by experience that I could take anything she said like that seriously. She never seemed to be off base in that realm. The event made a big impression on Rhonda and me. While we didn't know how or when the answer would take place, we understood that Grandma's prayer was significant."

Many years later Jim mentioned the instance to Uncle Bobby. It was then that Jim's uncle told him the rest of the story. "When you left, I asked Mama what she meant when she said, 'You've got it.' She looked straight at me and answered, 'One, two, maybe three.'"

Jim was deeply touched by his grandma's spiritual perception at a time when her body was but a shell, and her mind was almost completely gone. "Grandma died within a year or two of our visit to Florida, and our first child was not born until six years later. Although there seemed to be little life left in the grandma I had known, she evidently had still been able to communicate to the Lord," said Jim. "She knew when God had received her request, and she understood his answer. She no longer knew me, but she still knew how to pray!" In time God came to give Jim and Rhonda three children.

Pray for Comfort

Hear my cry, O God;

attend unto my prayer.

—Psalm 61:1

Home Before Dark

From her youth, Oma had a heart for the Lord, but her spiritual growth deepened over time, and her primary prayer ministry happened in her upper years—growing more intense after she became a widow at sixty-four years old. Her husband, Martin, died at seventy-one from a major stroke and complications from diabetes. For a time, Oma became very depressed, but she turned to the Lord, and he brought her out of that melancholy. She devoted the remainder of her life primarily to praying and reading her Bible. During that time, Oma's daughter, Elinor, returned to Miami. She lived with her mother for the next nineteen years.

"During those years, Mother's personal communion with God grew more intense," said Elinor. "She spent most of her time helping people over the phone and interceding for them. She regularly took prayer needs to the Throne of Grace—spending hours a day praying with an open Bible in her lap."

Then in her late seventies, Oma began having strokes. Eventually she lost some mental capacity, and her ability to pray diminished. It was then that Wayne suggested Elinor and their mother move up to Downers Grove, Illinois, where he was pastoring. Oma and Elinor lived up north for about six years. When Oma was eighty-nine and still in Downers Grove, she fell and broke her hip and was never able to walk again. Elinor was no longer able to take care of her mother, so Elinor and her brothers decided it would be good for their mother to go back to Florida to live with Bobby and his wife, Rosemary, in their mobile home.

When Bobby first took his mother, she was very upset with her adult children. She had been content living with Elinor, and she did not like this sudden change. Her children explained to her that it was best as Elinor was not able to take care of her mother and hold an outside job at the same time. For a short while their mother was unhappy, and she struggled with her attitude. Then one night about a month after the move, Bobby woke up and heard his mother talking to someone in the living room.

Assuring himself that his mother was okay, he chose not to confront her at the time.

The next morning, Bobby inquired of his mother, “Who were you talking to during the night?”

“You know that *good fellow*? He came and talked to me last night about my unhappiness with you and Elinor. He said I am wrong and that I shouldn't be angry—I should be happy. He said he wasn't going to come back and talk to me about it again.”

From that point on Oma reflected the joy of the Lord once again. Although she could no longer speak the name of Jesus, she spoke of him in her own way by calling him that *good fellow*. Even if most of the time she did not recognize her family by name, she still knew who Jesus was and could tell others all about him. And up until the final year of her life, she still made an effort to pray for people.

One morning about four years after his mother came to live with him, Bobby called his sister and brother to give them the news that their mother had gone to heaven. Rosemary had been feeding Oma cereal and singing “Jesus Loves Me” to her. “Mom tried to sing along, but she just wasn't able,” Bobby said. “She just closed her eyes and was gone.”

Oma had prayed for years, “Lord, take me home before dark.” She wanted to live for God and to be able to pray “until the lights went out.” Then she would be ready to go home to heaven. Since her health had failed so much during her last years, Elinor questioned whether that was a request God had not seen fit to honor. But Bobby reminded his sister that their mother was still joyful even to the moment of her death at ninety-three. And although she did not recognize people by then, she had been able to pray in a simple way and was still aware of God's presence. Monka, their mother's older sister had also died at the age of ninety-three, but in contrast, Monka's last three years had been spent lying in bed in a fetal position.

A note found written in Oma's Bible said, "Death is only a harmless shadow for us." Oma Van Gelderen died with the joy of the Lord on her countenance and "that good fellow" on her lips. "Bobby has a point," Elinor decided. "Even though Mother's health declined over time, she never lost her love for the Lord or her joy in singing the old hymns. She lived for God even to the point when there was very little physical strength left within her," Elinor said. Perhaps God did indeed take Mother home before dark."

Six years short of a century after her birth, Oma's earthly life ended as humbly as it began. But in the intervening years, she grew as an intercessor, a woman of faith who understood that God answers prayer. And because of God's faithfulness in responding to those prayers, people who were privileged to come in contact with Oma's intercession for them often witnessed miraculous intervention from God. Oma left nothing in the way of a physical estate. But her life was rich in what really mattered—a regular and effective communion with God. Today Oma would be thrilled at what God is doing in her family. But her family believes they are who they are because of the gift she gave them—her legacy of praying in faith.

But godliness with contentment is great gain. For we brought nothing into this world, and it is certain we can carry nothing out. And having food and raiment let us be therewith content. But they that will be rich fall into temptation and a snare, and into many foolish and hurtful lusts, which drown men in destruction and perdition. For the love of money is the root of all evil: which while some coveted after, they have erred from the faith, and pierced themselves through with many sorrows. But thou, O man of God, flee these things; and follow after righteousness, godliness, faith, love, patience, meekness. Fight the good fight of faith, lay hold on eternal life, whereunto thou art also called, and hast professed a good profession before many witnesses. –1 Timothy 6:6-12.

Pray with Expectation

But as for me, my prayer is unto thee, O LORD, in an acceptable time: O God, in the multitude of thy mercy hear me, in the truth of thy salvation.

—Psalm 69:13

Three Connected Truths Concerning Prayer

Adapted from a Message by John R. Van Gelderen

The Biblical Basis for My Grandmother's Prayers

God can teach any Christian who is willing, what it is to know the witness of the Spirit, and that it is a fact, not based upon a feeling. It is the knowledge that the Scriptures talk about in Romans 8:16, "The Spirit itself beareth witness with our spirit, that we are the children of God."

My grandmother, Oma Jacobs Van Gelderen, grew to understand this truth, and she became marked as a woman who walked by faith and not by sight. When the Spirit of God stirred her through his Word, she didn't miss it. When she had finished praying over a specific need, she often clapped her hands and exclaimed, "I've got it!" It is important for us to understand that all Christians can have it, if we first grasp hold of biblical truths concerning prayer. We begin by understanding that there are three connected truths concerning prayer: divine purposes, scriptural promises, and believing prayer (accessing the promises by faith).

Divine Purposes

God has a sovereign will. In that we mean that he has the full unlimited right and power to do whatever he chooses to do. We know this is true because the Bible says in 1 John 5 that if we ask anything according to God's will, he will hear us. Yet through the Lord's Prayer, Jesus taught his disciples to pray that God's will be done on earth as it is in heaven. Why did he ask them to pray in this manner? Because God's will was not being done on earth. So even though God rules the universe and has a sovereign will, he has set up creation so that his will is not automatic.

S. D. Gordon's *Quiet Talks on Prayer* was my grandmother's favorite book on prayer. Gordon says there are only two wills—God's will and Satan's will. What about man's will? Man's will lines up either with God's will or with Satan's will. Consider the following Scripture as we show that God's will is not automatic: "For this is good and acceptable in the sight of God, our Savior, who will have all men to be saved, and to come unto the knowledge of the truth," I Timothy 2:3–4. It is clear from this passage that it is God's will that all men be saved. Yet not all are saved. And just as it is possible to miss God's will concerning salvation, it is possible for children of God to miss God's will for their lives. His will is not inevitable. How then can God's will be done on earth as it is in heaven?

Scriptural Promises

God's divine purposes are revealed through scriptural promises, those exceeding great and precious promises found in only in God's Word. It is a matter of the Word and the Spirit. Romans 10:17 says, "So then faith cometh by hearing, and hearing by the word of God." We know that the Bible is loaded with promises. The question arises because we are not certain how we can know if we can stand on a particular promise for a given occasion?

The convincer is the Holy Spirit. There are times when we hear a message preached, and suddenly the Spirit of God opens our understanding. The illumination of the Word is poured out, and it comes alive in us. The Spirit is convincing us of the reality of those words. This is the evidence or what we will call the convincement. It is the Word giving evidence that we can not only believe, but that we can follow through with a course of action. That convincement is what we need in order to exercise faith. It is the work of the Holy Spirit that begins to open our eyes, to pour the light in, and to make us understand. He gives us evidence because he knows we are going to need it. When the Spirit of God stirs us through his Word, we must not miss it. This is walking by faith.

Believing Prayer

God is the sovereign of the universe. He is in control, but he has so designed it that in order to obtain his promises we must possess faith. While prayer is not the only expression of faith, it is a major expression of it. That is because prayer is not the issue; rather, faith is the issue. Prayer expresses faith. God's purposes revealed through his promises must be obtained by faith. This is how God chose to do it!

In what has been called the Hall of Faith chapter, Hebrews gives us this beautiful phrase: "Who through faith . . . obtained promises," Hebrews 11:33. Here we see that the promises have to be accessed. We get them through faith. They are not automatic. We see it also in James 4:2, "Ye have not because ye ask not." We recognize that the following verse says that we ask and don't receive because we ask amiss. However, when we connect the truths—divine purposes, scriptural promises, and believing prayer—when we have divine purposes revealed through scriptural promises, we are not talking about asking amiss. When we talk about divine purposes revealed by scriptural promises, then at that point the only reason we do not obtain is simply because we have not asked!

One of the greatest regrets we will have when we get to heaven will be when we discover all that God would have done and given. It was his will, but we did not ask, and consequently we never received. First John 5:14–15 says, "And this is the confidence that we have in him, that, if we ask any thing according to his will, he heareth us: And if we know that he hear us, whatsoever we ask, we know that we have the petitions that we desired of him."

I saw this truth exemplified in my grandmother Oma's prayers. Once the Spirit of God gave her convincement, she did not stop right there as if it were a done deal. And she did not appear to become disillusioned. When results did not happen immediately, she did not question whether God was true to his Word. Oma understood that she did not have because she had not asked yet. She understood the biblical truth that the Holy Spirit's convincement was the groundwork or basis for her asking in confidence rather than wishful thinking. As we think about the meaning of the word promise—that a particular thing will come about—we can see that a promise in itself reveals the purpose of the one giving it. However, the flip side is that a promise demands faith from the one receiving it. Our heavenly Father is waiting for his child to say, "Daddy, you said you would—you gave me your Word. You promised! Now, when are you going to do it?"

Divine purposes are like checks in God's checkbook—they are filled out but not signed. Scriptural promises are like signed checks in God's checkbook. Believing prayer is like cashing the check. We understand that a check is no benefit to us until we take it to the bank and exchange it for cash. God's promises work much the same way. It is an amazing truth that God has chosen to accomplish his purposes through the believing partnership of his people. In Ezekiel chapter 36 God says he will do this for his people, and he will do that for his people. He lists several glorious promises, and then at the end of it all, he says in verse 37, "Thus saith the Lord God; I will yet for this be enquired of by the house of Israel, to do it for them; I will increase them with men like a flock." In other words, God says, "Here is my purpose; here is my promise, but I am not going to do it until they ask." God wants us to come into union with him through faith—through dependence upon the reality of his words. With this in mind, we can categorize prayer into three major phases. First there is praying to the promise, then there is the prayer of faith, and finally there is praying from the promise through to victory.

Praying to the Promise

There was a time when certain Christian groups talked about *praying through*. Today that term may cause the average Christian to scratch their head and wonder what this term is all about. However, once we understand how God's promises are linked to our faith, praying through begins to make sense. It is the practice of praying to the promise until we are convinced that the promise will hold for this specific occasion. It is as if God is holding the answer out for us to receive. The prayer of faith is simply asking and taking. It is a transaction with God.

Praying to the promise is praying until we see the evidence through Holy Spirit convincement—that is praying through until the Holy Spirit has convinced us. We know God can meet the need, but we do not know if he will. So we must pray that God will give us his mind on the subject at hand. When he does that, and he convinces us of words that reveal his will, then we can pray the prayer of faith. Praying from the promise through the victory is prayer that is based on that transaction. It is affirming what God has given in the spiritual realm and trusting him to manifest that answer in the physical realm. I saw this lived out in my grandmother. I think it can safely be said that Oma Van Gelderen was a woman who prayed through!

James A. Stewart was a man used of God in some tremendous revivals before and after World War II in Eastern Europe. His wife says in his biography that when he came to new regions, he would take the map and spread it across the bed. Then he would get on his knees. "God, here's a new need. Now, God, I know that you can meet the need—you are able, but I don't know if you will meet the need." Stewart then began to wrestle with God. He said that the greatest wrestling for him was the first phase—coming to understand the mind of the Lord. It was in that phase where he was seeking to discern, "What is God's will for this occasion?" It is understandable that this was Stewart's biggest hurdle, because he knew that once he had the evidence—the signed check—God would bring it to pass. All Stewart had to do at that juncture was to ask.

Understanding this very important truth concerning prayer now gives us clarity as to why so many prayers seemingly go unanswered. We do not pray in confidence because we do not take the time to get the mind of God in the first place. Once we get his mind on a particular matter, once we have the evidence, it is at that stage when we can grab hold of the horns of the altar as they say. We can pray, "God, these are your words. Holy Spirit you convinced us. Now, do not let your truth be mocked." We can say without apology, "God, you've got to do this!"

This is when praying gets bold. This is what Isaiah is talking about when God says, "You command me." It is not that we are trying to shove our will on God. In deepest reverence we can truly say it is a matter of pushing God's will on God. And that is the difference. This is not "name it and claim it" praying. It is a matter of finding out what God wants, and then saying, "God, this is what you want. This is what you said. This is what you convinced me of for this situation, for this occasion. God, you've got to come through."

Praying from the Promise Through to Victory

To confirm that God's will is not automatic, let us look at his will concerning salvation. The Bible says that God is not willing that any should perish, but that all should come to repentance. "The Lord is not slack concerning his promise, as some men count slackness, but is longsuffering toward us, not willing that any should perish, but that all should come to repentence," 2 Peter 3:9.

Now, there's a difference between being convinced of that as a general truth versus being convinced of that for a particular person—a difference between being convinced in a general sense versus those times when the Holy Spirit convinces us, and we can stand on that Word for that person on that occasion at that time. This truth is clear throughout the Bible. In 1 Kings 17, Elijah tells King Ahab,

"As the Lord God of Israel liveth, before whom I stand, there shall not be dew nor rain these years, but according to my word."

Now, that was a bold statement for Elijah to make. Can you imagine barging into the Oval Office and announcing to the president that it is not going to rain in the United States of America until you say so? Well, it was most likely even more bold back when Elijah confronted King Ahab. Was Elijah out of his mind, or did he have a foundation for his boldness? First Kings does not tell us. It says Elijah went in and boldly made the announcement, but it does not tell us what his foundation for faith was based on. However, when we turn to the New Testament and go to the book of James, we learn there is more to the story. James 5:17 states, "Elias was a man subject to like passions as we are, and he prayed earnestly that it might not rain: and it rained not on the earth by the space of three years and six months."

Elijah prayed earnestly that it might not rain. That part of the story is not found in 1 Kings. While it might be implied there, we read in James the confirmation that before Elijah went to the king, he had prayed earnestly. This brings up a dilemma. A lot of people pray earnestly and still do not see things happen. How did Elijah know it was the will of God and pray with confidence that this thing would happen? What was the foundation for Elijah's faith? Neither 1 Kings nor James 5 tells us the answer to this question. However, Deuteronomy and Leviticus do tell us. And Elijah would have been familiar with the first five books of the Old Testament. In Deuteronomy 28 and Leviticus 26, God shares promises that are explicitly dealing with what Elijah was facing. They are also stated both positively and negatively in Deuteronomy 11. God said in Deuteronomy 11:13–15, "And it shall come to pass, if ye shall hearken diligently unto my commandments which I command you this day, to love the Lord your God, and to serve him with all your heart and with all your soul, That I will give you the rain of your land in his due season, the first rain and the latter rain, that thou mayest gather in thy corn, and thy wine, and thine oil. And I will send grass in thy fields for thy cattle, that thou mayest eat and be full." So on the positive side God is saying, if you love me and serve me with your whole heart, I am going to give you rain. Your needs will be met.

Now, let's look at the negative side. In verses 16–17, God says, "Take heed to yourselves, that your heart be not deceived, and ye turn aside, and serve other gods, and worship them; And then the Lord's wrath be kindled against you, and he shut up the heaven, that there be no rain, and that the land yield not her fruit; and lest ye perish quickly from off the good land which the Lord giveth you."

Let us think this through. James 5 tells us Elijah prayed earnestly that it might not rain. Keep in mind that the promises of the Old Testament were clear concerning this event. If the people loved God, he would make it rain, and they would have their needs met. If they turned away from him and bowed down and worshiped other gods, then there would be no rain, and their needs would not be met. Now we must ask a very important question. Was Israel at a place in their history in which they loved and served God? No, they had turned aside and were serving Baal. They were in full-blown idolatry and apostasy. And God had told them that if they did that, he would stop the rain.

Why did Elijah have to pray earnestly that it might not rain? Because it was still raining! Israel had been in idolatry for years, and God had said when they went in this direction, he would shut up the heavens and send no rain. There we have his promise that reveals his purpose. The important truth to remember is that it had to be accessed by believing prayer. This is why James 5 tells us that Elijah prayed earnestly that it might not rain. The promise was there, but somebody had to obtain it. Most of the time when we think about promises, we think of them in a positive light. But in this case, Elijah was grabbing hold of a negative promise, not so he could "bash heads," but so the nation would be awakened back to God.

God sent the fire when Elijah prayed on Mt. Carmel. At that time the people briefly turned back to God when they cried out, "Jehovah he is the God." So there is a sense where

Elijah could have stood on the positive promise based on this brief turning back. But beyond that, according to 1 Kings 18, the Word of the Lord came to Elijah, and God told him it was going to rain. What did Elijah do? He prayed for rain because he understood what we do not—this promise revealed God's purpose, but it was not going to happen until somebody asked for it. He sent his servant to see if there was a cloud. No cloud. He prayed again seven times. He kept praying, not because he believed God *could* send the rain, but because he believed that God *would* send the rain. That is the kind of praying my grandmother did. She got hold ofthe Word of God, and God brought it to pass because she accessed it by faith!

Those who were closest to Grandma often witnessed when she reached that point in which she had prayed through. Suddenly the burden was gone. God had heard, and the manifest answer was right around the corner. This is what my grandmother meant when she exclaimed, "I've got it!" She had begun by taking time to get the mind of God. She had asked him to give her the convincement she needed so she could pray through and see him glorified. The truths in these scriptural principles are not only for a select few, they are for all Christians. When we pray the prayer of faith, we see results! This is the prayer that makes a difference.

CPSIA information can be obtained
at www.ICGtesting.com
Printed in the USA
LVOW13s2309121216
517005LV00031B/931/P

9 780997 495317